D0363953

© LADYBIRD BOOKS LTD 1975

All rights reserved. No part of this publication may be reproduced, stored in a retrieval system, or transmitted in any form or by any means, electronic, mechanical, photo-copying, recording or otherwise, without the prior consent of the copyright owner.

Bonnie Prince Charlie

by L. DU GARDE PEACH,
O.B.E., M.A., Ph.D., D.Litt.

with illustrations by
ROGER HALL

Ladybird Books Ltd Loughborough

BONNIE PRINCE CHARLIE

Bonnie Prince Charlie or, to give him his full name, Charles Edward Louis Philippe Casimir Stuart, was born in Rome a few days after Christmas, 1720. Known as the 'Young Pretender', he was considered by the followers of his grandfather, the exiled King James II, as the rightful heir to the united thrones of England, Scotland and Ireland. His father had been the 'Old Pretender', which meant that each of them had pretences or rights to the crown. When Prince Charles Edward was born in 1720, the Hanoverian, George the First, who spoke only a few words of English, was on the throne.

Prince Charles Edward was a bright, intelligent and attractive boy. Educated at his father's court without any ordinary schooling, he spoke English, French and Italian fluently. He was a general favourite; the fact that at the age of only thirteen he was present at the siege of the Italian port of Gaeta shows that he was as brave as he was adventurous. He was to give ample proof of it later.

He did more. He brought trouble to Scotland for generations to come, but at the same time inspired the Scottish nation. The story of what is known as the 'Forty-Five' is one of heroism, loyalty, patriotism, and the devotion of a people as poor as any in Europe. Any one of them could have claimed a reward of thirty thousand pounds for betraying their young Prince. None did.

It is a story which is no credit to England, but which is honoured and cherished by Scottish men and women the world over.

Prince Charles Edward at the Siege of Gaeta

0 7214 0421 9

The Stuarts had been Kings of Scotland for centuries before James VI of Scotland succeeded Elizabeth I in 1603 as James I of England. In other 'Ladybird' Books in this series the somewhat complicated and confused history may be read of why a Scottish Stuart King should become the Ruler of Scotland's enemy. Queen Anne, the great-grand-daughter of James I of England, was in effect the last English monarch of the House of Stuart in the direct line. She was followed by George of Hanover, a German, whose grandmother, a daughter of James I, was his only link with the Stuarts. It was a distant and feeble link, and the Scottish patriots refused to recognise him at all.

James II, exiled from England in 1689, died in France in 1701, and an attempt by a party of patriotic Jacobites to crown his son in London as James III so provoked the citizens that those taking part had to flee for their lives. The people of London had not forgotten James II.

The Scots, like so many nations inhabiting bleak mountainous country where life is harsh, were a warlike people at that time, determined, hardy, able to withstand extremes of heat and cold, and utterly without fear. In Stuart times, too, they were desperately poor. Intensely proud and owing allegiance to their Clan Chieftains to the death, they hated the alien rule of England.

Such a people are apt to be fiercely revengeful. Feuds between one Clan and another are kept alive for generations, and to this day there are Highland Clansmen who refuse to have anything to do with a member of the Clan Campbell. The reason for this, as we shall find, goes back to the 'Forty-Five'.

6   *The warlike Scots*

In 1745 such firearms as the Clansmen possessed were mostly old and much inferior in range to those of regular troops. But where every man depended upon himself for his own protection, they were skilled in their use, and made up for what they lacked in effective fire-power and discipline by reckless courage.

There had already been three attempts at throwing off the English domination. All had failed. The first was in 1708 when some French ships sailed from Dunkirk with a French force of 5,000 men, reached the Firth of Forth, and returned. The expedition had been very badly organised, and to add to other misfortunes, James became ill just as the ships were about to sail. Of all the things to delay an invasion, it was a case of measles.

The second attempt, in 1715, was equally unsuccessful, although it seemed for a while to promise well. The revolt was started by the Earl of Mar in Scotland and by an English Jacobite, the Earl of Derwentwater, in England. The Old Pretender landed at Peterhead in December, having been proclaimed earlier at Braemar as James VIII of Scotland and James III of England. Marching south some eighty miles to Scone, he hesitated. The Highlanders, hearing of the approach of a force under the Earl of Argyle, and disheartened by the indecisive result of a battle in November at Sheriffmuir, vanished into the mountains. James returned to France accompanied by the Earl of Mar, having achieved nothing.

Two years later, a Spanish naval expedition organised by the statesman Aberoni was scattered by a storm. Only two battered frigates reached the Hebridean Isle of Lewis.

The last two Spanish frigates approach the Isle of Lewis

In the year following the dispersal of the Spanish fleet, Prince Charles Edward was born in Rome, the son of James and the Polish Princess Clementina Sobieski, whom James had married the year before. Prince Charles was acclaimed by the Scottish Jacobites as the Prince of Wales, but never recognised as such by the English.

This is the romantic story of his invasion of England which was the fourth and last attempt by Scottish patriots to liberate their country from alien rule.

Today Scotland is visited every year by thousands of English holiday-makers. New and efficient roads, bus-services, bridges replacing old ferries, aerodromes and caravan sites, together with new hotels and accommodation for all kinds of sport from ski-ing to mountaineering, have opened up a country which even at the beginning of the present century was almost as wild as when the Clans marched south in 1745.

Many romances have been written round the history of the '45; many of them are nothing more than romantic legends. There are however two which, written by Scotsmen, give a vivid picture of the country from which the Clans came, and in which bewildered English soldiers sought hopelessly for Bonnie Prince Charlie. Almost every grim faced Highlander they met on the mountain tracks knew where he was; the English never did, until it was too late.

Waverley by Sir Walter Scott, and *Kidnapped* by Robert Louis Stevenson are familiar to many Scotsmen: English boys and girls who do not know the Scottish Highlands should read them if they wish to know the sort of country for which Scotsmen fought and died. *The Burning Cresset* by Howard Pease gives a good picture of the earlier rising of 1715.

Although brought up largely in France and Italy, Prince Charles Edward lived in a court fervently devoted to the cause of Jacobite Scottish nationalism. He never forgot that he was a Stuart, and a member of a Royal House. Romantic, adventurous, trained in arms, and encouraged by a French King ready to help anyone to harm England, he was determined to win back Scotland for the Scots. He wrote that he would 'conquer or die'.

In 1744 he was twenty-four, an age at which any young man of spirit is eager for action. When a crown is to be gained by success, the inducement to take almost any risk becomes irresistible. Prince Charles Edward had no intention of resisting it.

Money, ships, arms, ammunition, and above all, men: these were the needs of Prince Charles before he could think of invasion. Not that he was doubtful. He was ready to sail to Scotland with, as he said, only his personal servant to accompany him. Between them they would raise the Lion Flag of Scotland, and every Scot would rally to his call. He had good reason for thinking so. There were many thousands of Scots, both in Scotland and in England, who drank the King's health every day and they did not mean King George! Because it was high treason even to name King James, they passed their glasses over a bowl of water as they gave the toast of 'The King!' They were drinking to 'The King over the water!'

To this day there are to be found in many Scottish mansions wine-glasses inscribed with the Stuart crest; many a Scot risked his life by using them.

Drinking to 'The King over the water'

Unfortunately for the high hopes of Prince Charles Edward, many Scots were ready to drink a romantic toast to the exiled King 'over the water', but thought twice when it came to open rebellion. King George was nearer than King James in France. To the Lowlanders just north of the Border, he was much nearer than to the Highlanders in the remote mountainous regions of the north.

The Highlanders were for the most part descendants of Gaelic tribes. They were always ready to fight, because fighting meant plunder. The Celtic inhabitants of the Lowlands, more civilised and more given to trade, looked on the wild Highlanders as little better than brigands, and were reluctant to join any enterprise in which they were concerned. They feared that whatever happened, they would come off second best and they were probably right.

Prince Charles was to experience another disappointment. France was at war with England, and a French invasion had been planned to take place at the same time as the Scots' rising. The Prince had established a base at Gravelines, near Calais, and a French fleet was ready to sail with 7,000 troops commanded by the famous French Marshal, Saxe. The number of troops varies according to different accounts; there may have been double that number. However many there were, they were considerably discouraged by the appearance of a squadron of British warships; the French soldiers may not have been sorry when violent storms at sea caused the invasion to be cancelled!

The French troops disembarked and marched away and that was the end of the French help promised by Louis.

French troops disembarking

Prince Charles was still young enough not to be discouraged. Inspired by a burning patriotism, he was ready to risk anything and everything. The French ships being no longer available, he determined to organise an expedition himself, however small it had to be, with such money as he could raise. He sold all his jewels, and with the help of an Irish patriot, who probably hated the English as much as he did, he was able to obtain two small ships. These were *Du Teillay*, and an armed frigate, the *Elizabeth*. With a few Scottish patriots, 'Bonnie Prince Charlie' set sail from France on the 13th of July, 1745.

The two little ships were intercepted by the English man-o'-war *Lion*, and both were badly damaged in a short action. The frigate containing most of the arms and ammunition was obliged to return to France; Prince Charles and his companions, known as 'the Seven Men of Moidart', escaped. They reached the little island of Eriskay in the Hebrides, but finding little hope of active support, they set sail for the west coast of Inverness-shire.

Landing at Moidart on the 25th of July, they were met by the Macdonald, who, although he was very doubtful of success, was loyal to the Prince. When almost four weeks later, on the desolate marshy bay of Glenfinnan, the Standard was unfurled by the Duke of Atholl, and blessed by the Bishop of Morar, the most romantically reckless adventure in the history of Scotland had begun.

If it had succeeded, the whole history of Britain, even of Europe, might have been different. It failed, but remains an inspiration to generations of Scots for all time.

Raising the Standard at Glenfinnan

It was the 19th of August, 1745, a date never forgotten by Scotsmen, and commemorated by one of the loneliest monuments in the British Isles. Within a few days, more than a thousand men of the Clans Macdonald and Cameron had gathered. More were to join them later. The fighting spirit of the Highlanders, the personal charm of the young Stuart Prince, and the stupidity of the English Government were all on the side of the Scots. An English garrison of 3,000 soldiers, under the command of an officer so incompetent as almost to amount to imbecility, was at Stirling. To prevent the Scots from invading England from Glenfinnan on the west coast, he marched his little army a hundred miles northwards to Inverness.

If we look at a map of Scotland we find Inverness on the Moray Firth, on the east coast, forty miles further north than Glenfinnan in the west.

Not surprisingly when Prince Charles heard that the English soldiers had actually left the road to England open, he could scarcely believe it. He immediately did what must have infuriated the English Commander far away in Inverness; he marched east and captured Stirling.

If the English Commander was angry, the Government in England was frightened. The Prime Minister was a timid man named Pelham, who knew that there were thousands of Scots in England who hated King George. What was worse, almost the whole of the British Army was in Flanders, fighting the French, and the reputation of the Highland Clans was enough to frighten braver men than Pelham. The Government was soon to have ample cause to share the panic which was to follow in London.

"The English have gone to Inverness!"

We can imagine the excitement and wild rejoicing of the Highlanders when they found themselves in possession of the town from which the English soldiers had shortly before marched away northwards. The inhabitants cheered in the hope that the Clansmen would not loot the goods of fellow Scots who at least seemed to be their friends.

Their hopes were not entirely justified. Victory and loot went together in the minds of many if not all of the Highlanders. The citizens of Stirling rejoiced in the Scottish success, but they were not sorry when the Prince and his undisciplined followers left for Edinburgh.

In the meantime Sir John Cope, commanding the English Army in Inverness, had realised that if Edinburgh were to be saved, it was high time to return south. The march overland would take too long. Embarking his men, he sailed down the coast to Dunbar. Time was against him. On September 17th Edinburgh had been occupied amid scenes of wild enthusiasm, and Prince Charles was holding high revel in the Palace of Holyrood.

Cope did what he could. He marched to Prestonpans, a few miles east of Edinburgh, and prepared to give battle. His position was well chosen. In front was marshy ground behind which he thought he was safe from direct attack. If the Clansmen attempted to cross it, his cannon would be able to shoot them down; for any who reached the dry land, he had two thousand trained soldiers waiting. Posting sentries in the correct military fashion, the English lay down to get what sleep they could. They got very little.

Two thousand English soldiers prepare for battle

The early morning of September the 17th was dark and the mist was so thick that the English sentries were unable to see more than a few feet in any direction. In such weather they were useless. The Highlanders were accustomed to it and, gathering by Clans about three o'clock, they moved silently down towards the swamp. A local laird, named Robert Anderson, led the way by a little-known path through the marshy ground. It was rough and broken, and it was difficult to keep in touch with the men in front.

Moving silently through the mist, the Highlanders made their way round the left flank of the English line. They were now on more or less flat stubble fields, behind the position thought by Cope to be impregnable. The mists thinned as the sky began to grow lighter.

Suddenly a sentry heard something suspicious and challenged. He fired his musket in the direction of the sound. As the shot rang out, the startled English sprang up to find the Clansmen already on the move behind them. Almost before they knew what was happening, the wild-looking Highlanders were amongst them. Unable to reload, those who managed to fix their clumsy bayonets found that a weapon six feet long was useless in a crowded mass of brawny men, stabbing and slashing with short claymores used with savage efficiency.

The English Dragoons, mounting their plunging chargers, were seized with panic and galloped away; the infantry, appalled by the savage violence and utter reck-lessness of the charging Clansmen, broke and fled in disorder. One impetuous charge was enough. The battle lasted seven minutes.

Fierce Clansmen attack

The news that regular English troops had been so disastrously defeated caused a panic in London. Terrified fugitives from the battle at Prestonpans had galloped south with stories of the wild fury of the Clansmen. Nothing, they said, could withstand them; disciplined regulars had thrown away their weapons and run like frightened sheep. The story grew as it spread. Panic-stricken citizens expected that in a matter of days savage Highlanders would be in the streets of London. Everyone would be murdered!

Thousands of nervous citizens besieged the Banks until the only coins which remained were sixpenny pieces. Soon there were no more of these either.

Pelham was not the man to cope with such a situation. His Cabinet was composed of men even less capable than himself. The war with France meant that very few trained soldiers remained in England. Marshal Wade, the most trusted English commander of the day, when asked for his opinion, said that England could not be defended.

The Scots were jubilant. One furious charge by the Camerons had won the battle almost before it had started. Knowing nothing of the military resources in England, and less of the discipline of a trained professional army under capable officers, they believed that any battle could be won in the same way as that of Prestonpans. It was true that Edinburgh Castle still held out: stone walls cannot be overcome by a single desperate charge. The garrison even fired an occasional contemptuous shot. As it did no damage, and Edinburgh was completely in their hands, the Scots, intent on other matters, took no notice of it.

"England cannot be defended!"

The capture of Edinburgh, and the proclamation by Prince Charles of King James VIII of Scotland at the Market Cross, encouraged a number of hesitating Clans to join the Scottish forces. Prince Charles now had about six thousand Highlanders under his command. The only thing which prevented him from marching south through undefended England to London was that the Clansmen were not under his command when it came to neglecting other interests.

Plunder was for the Highland Clansmen the natural result of winning a battle, and Edinburgh was the richest prize many of them had ever seen. It was theirs, and such an opportunity might never occur again. They were ready as patriotic Scots to cheer a Scottish King, but now that Scotland was a free Kingdom again, why bother with England? In vain Prince Charles assured them that there was infinitely more and richer plunder to be won in England; they preferred to make sure of what they already had, rather than risk it all by going after more.

Consequently it was not until weeks later, on November the 1st, that he was able to persuade them to march south. He had now about five thousand Clansmen on foot, and something under a thousand mounted. It was a formidable fighting force, but it was now too late. A month or so earlier there would have been nobody to defend England against a rapid march on London.

Again it was the Highlanders inbred view that fighting meant raids in the cause of vengeance or plunder or both which doomed the invasion to failure. As they advanced into England, the Prince's army melted away; more and more Clansmen left for home, driving English cattle before them.

Proclaiming the new king in Edinburgh

The five or six weeks wasted by the Highlanders in Edinburgh gave the English Government time to recall the Duke of Cumberland and a number of Guards and Infantry battalions from the Continent. The Militia, part-time soldiers similar to the modern Territorials, were called up. Marshal Wade, who would seem to have recovered his nerve, marched north at the head of an army. The Duke of Cumberland was on the way to Lichfield with more regular troops. The citizens of London began to feel a little safer.

Meanwhile the Prince, now with more than six thousand Highlanders, marched on Carlisle, ninety miles south. The roads, which were poor at any time, were deep in snow. This was the sort of weather which was normal to the Highlanders. After a short siege, Carlisle surrendered, and the unwelcome Clansmen marched on to Penrith and Preston.

There was little opposition, except from those who objected to losing their goods or cattle. There were many deserters, but few recruits. The Prince had hoped that the people of the north would flock to his banner, but it was not until he reached Manchester that even a meagre two or three hundred volunteers declared for the Stuart cause.

Sir Walter Scott describes the reception given to the straggling column. 'No man cried "God bless him!" The mob stared and listened, heartless, stupefied, and dull. They gazed with astonishment, mixed with horror and aversion, at the wild appearance, unknown language, and singular garb of the Scottish Clans. Their scanty numbers, apparent deficiency in discipline, and poverty of equipment, seemed certain tokens of the calamitous termination of their rash undertaking.' Simple peace-loving citizens wisely left them alone.

The Clansmen were regarded with great distrust on their way south

28

As Prince Charles and his men marched south, Marshal Wade waited hopefully to intercept them at Newcastle. Today, armies hundreds of miles apart are in instant communication by wireless. It is difficult to realise that the English commander at Newcastle did not know that Prince Charles was already scores of miles to the south of him on the way to England! The Duke of Cumberland was well out of the way with his 12,000 men, comfortably billeted in Lichfield.

At Manchester, believed to be strongly in favour of the Jacobite cause, the disappointingly few volunteers later became the Manchester Regiment of today. Apart from this small addition to the Prince's little army, Manchester's welcome was restricted to some illuminations and a gift of two thousand pounds, worth a great deal more then than it would be today.

Derby was reached on December the 4th. The news that the wild Highlanders were now only 125 miles from London produced a panic which spread to the Palace itself. George II was said to have ordered his bags to be packed with a view to returning to Hanover if the Prince came any nearer. Although 30,000 men were guarding London at Finchley, George felt that Hanover, with the English Channel in between, would be more conducive to his peace of mind.

Neither King George in London nor Marshal Wade, now fifteen miles west of York, knew what was happening in Derby. All they knew was that Prince Charles had taken the town, and that no regular English troops had yet been able to withstand the savage fury of the charge of the Clans. If it had been in their power to listen to the conference between the Prince and his officers, they might have viewed things differently.

George II prepares to leave

In Derby a group of Highland Chieftains were gathered about the handsome young Prince. Their expressions were those of brave and gallant men forced to a reluctant decision. Led by Lord George Murray, who had fought in the Jacobite risings of 1715 and 1719, they realised that the support they had received in England was not enough. To advance further, with the few men still left to them, would be madness.

We can imagine the scene. The Prince is young and the recklessness of an adventurous dash on London stirs his blood. He would risk everything on sudden surprise and the romantic tradition of the Stuarts. Once in London, the people would remember Charles II and the grim Puritans of Oliver Cromwell. His welcome, the welcome of a gay Stuart King again, would be what it was for Charles.

Lord George Murray shakes his head sadly. England and the English have changed. So far the Clansmen have charged and won against small detachments of the English Army. But England could put a hundred thousand disciplined professional troops in the field. Three thousand Highlanders remained with the Prince. The further they got from Scotland, the greater would be the temptation to return with what they already had.

Which of them was right? Once on the throne, a romantic young King might have seemed more attractive than a dull German running for his life. Who knows? It was a desperate venture, but desperate ventures have succeeded before now. There was no doubt that this was an adventure, with every argument against it. It was a bitter decision for the Prince who had come so far. But he recognised its necessity. On December the 6th the retreat began.

The retreat was a more dangerous undertaking for the Clansmen than had been the advance. Weary, often hungry, and most of them carrying items of plunder which they were reluctant to throw away, they were still feared by the civilians. A Scottish wolf at bay is worse than one intent only on escape. The Clansman who strayed from the main body was doomed, but the column of ragged, half-starved men was left alone.

The Dragoons under the Duke of Cumberland were close on their heels. Occasionally they dared an attack on an isolated rearguard, only to be driven off by the fearless charges of the embittered Highlanders. Such raids and short actions continued as the column struggled along some of the worst roads in England. It was not until after the Border had been crossed that the retreating Scots turned on their ruthless pursuers at Falkirk.

This was on January the 17th, during an unsuccessful attempt to take Stirling Castle. Finding an English force under General Hawley closing in on them, the Clansmen attacked, charging with the reckless fury which the English soldiery had come to dread. The unhappy General and his men were driven from the field in disorder.

This success again raised the hopes of the Prince, but his more experienced Clansmen realised that the reserves which the English could call upon amounted to many thousands. The siege of Stirling was raised and the retreat continued, but the end had not yet come. More Clans were declaring for the Jacobites and Prince Charles. They had won every engagement so far, and the Scots of the far north still hoped for an independence they had once enjoyed.

A lone Highlander attacked by resentful English civilians

The Duke of Cumberland, with a true German's preference for comfort, occupied Aberdeen. He remained there until April, enjoying such hospitality as the citizens were prepared to offer.

The Clansmen dispersed to their Highland fastnesses with such booty as they had been able to carry during the long march from Derby. The small number which remained with the Prince did not regard themselves as a beaten army. Even the growing numbers of regular soldiers in Scotland, now amounting to thirty thousand, did not unduly discourage them. They had seen English soldiers turn and run on many occasions, and had a poor opinion of their fighting qualities.

The Clan Chiefs took a different view. Prince Charles would have attacked, but Lord George Murray knew that small successes were not enough. Unless a French army came to their help, no hope remained. Courage and patriotism could not in the end prevail against numbers amounting to ten, or if necessary a hundred, to one. The Scots could die, but they could not win.

Caution was not in the character of Bonnie Prince Charlie. If it had been, he would not have become the hero of a legend of gay adventure. The Scots as a people are generally regarded as dour rather than gay, but they respect and appreciate courage and determination. A lost cause is never lost for a Scot. Many people have owed final success to members of this grimly efficient race, not least their English neighbours. Unfortunately, as is the case with many peoples composed of clans or tribes owing allegiance to none but their tribal chiefs, they find it difficult to combine peacefully.

A Clansman returns home

The Prince was persuaded to fall back to Inverness. From here it would be easy to take refuge amongst the mountains and treacherous peat-bogs of the Highlands. The English soldiers would be at such a disadvantage that they would hesitate to follow. In the Clan country of the far north and west, a new army could be recruited. The English were frightened; their troops, many of them German mercenaries, had no interest in the struggle. Their German King George was heartily disliked. Finally, why not wait for better weather?

Whether the Prince was convinced or not, we do not know. When, early in April, he heard that the Duke of Cumberland had 8,000 picked troops under orders to march north, he quickly made up his mind. The Clans were mustered, and against the advice of Lord George Murray, the Prince decided to fight. If this English army could be destroyed by the charge of the Clans, as previous ones had been, a new Scottish force would be easy to recruit; if the battle went the other way, it would not be required.

The action began badly for the Prince. Cumberland's men were halted for the night near Nairn, on the Moray Firth, sixteen miles east of Inverness. The Prince decided on a night attack, such as had proved so successful at Prestonpans.

Today the motorist drives along a first-class road from Inverness to Nairn in a quarter of an hour: in 1746 there was no first-class road. The mere track which existed was difficult to follow on a dark, bitterly cold night. A north-east wind with hail and wet snow blew directly in their faces. The frozen Highlanders returned to Inverness.

Struggling along the cold road to Nairn

The morning of April the 16th dawned with the same north-east wind bringing sleet and snow. The Prince roused his men after a few hours indifferent rest, and took up a position on Culloden Moor. The intention was to cover the road over which the English must advance towards Inverness, but it was not ideal for defence.

The Highlanders had not long to wait. Soon the English came in sight. They were better fed, better armed, and, if not better led, were disciplined and well supported by the primitive artillery of the day. They quickly formed up in long lines in the way in which they were drilled to receive a cavalry charge. The front line knelt with the second and third lines standing close behind them. Bayonets were fixed, and a hedge of bristling steel opposed the enemy.

The Clansmen charged, firing their pistols as they ran. The English cannon had been loaded with what was known as grape-shot, so called because it consisted of a handful of lead balls the size of grapes. These scattered like the pellets from a sporting cartridge. The effect on the Clansmen, massed together as they ran, was terrible. Musketry fire added to the casualties inflicted on the attackers, who could do little in return until they came to hand-to-hand fighting.

Very few reached the English lines. Those that did so flung themselves on the hedge of bayonets, ready to die rather than admit defeat. When the Dragoons of Cumberland's army, until then held back in reserve, charged on the flank of the broken and stricken Clans, the battle was lost.

The Clansmen charged in vain

It was after the Battle of Culloden that the Duke of Cumberland earned, and deserved, the name of 'the Butcher'. He ordered hundreds of prisoners to be shot, and his soldiers were permitted, and may well have been ordered, to cut down all fugitives with savage cruelty. This terrible policy of brutal murder was continued for many months in the Scottish glens. Farmsteads were burnt, and cattle and sheep killed or stolen. The wearing of the Scottish national dress, with its distinctive Clan tartan, was enough to condemn a man to be hanged. The diabolic cruelty of this son of a King of England was a disgrace to the country which permitted him to live in it.

The adventurous evasions and hairbreadth escapes of Bonnie Prince Charlie between April the 16th and September the 20th are amongst the most romantic episodes in the history of the British Isles. For five months, hunted by hundreds of armed men and with a price of thirty thousand pounds on his head, he lived a legend which will be remembered long after the Battle of Culloden is forgotten.

When no hope of victory remained, the Prince rode south with a few officers along the high ground southeast of Loch Ness to Fort Augustus and on to Arisaig. For four days and nights they slept where they could and ate fish caught in the rivers and lochs.

The track which they had followed on horseback came to an end. Now they were in wild, rough mountainous country, hungry and on foot. Their spirits were not raised by passing Glenfinnan, where the flag had been so hopefully raised little more than a year before.

The track had come to an end

Prince Charles remained at Arisaig for the next four days. They were four days of adverse news which would have broken the heart of anyone other than this gay young Prince. From his most loyal follower and trusted commander, Lord George Murray, a letter was brought to him; in it Lord George blamed him for the disaster at Culloden, recklessly ordered against the advice of all his officers; it ended with Lord George's decision not to continue his command of the Prince's forces.

This was not the only serious blow to his hopes of which Prince Charles learnt whilst at Arisaig. He had thought to find a safe hiding place with loyal Clansmen on the Isle of Skye. When he heard that they had turned against him, he decided to cross to the Hebrides. On one of these bleak, almost uninhabited, islands he might be safe until he could find a ship to take him to France.

An old sailor, Donald, would be able to find an eight-oared boat, but he reported that the Minch, the stretch of water between the mainland and the Hebrides, was patrolled by English ships. To make the crossing without being seen and captured would be almost impossible.

The sky was clouding over and out to sea the white horses were riding the waves. A storm was blowing up, and until it had died down, Donald was against putting out to sea in an open boat, but English soldiers were reported nearing Arisaig. It was a choice between the risk of being drowned at sea, or taken prisoner on land. No storm, however dangerous, could be as savagely cruel as the Duke of Cumberland. They sailed on the evening tide.

Crossing to the Hebrides in a storm

It was a wild night, and a wind of gale force drove the little boat far to the westward. It was fortunate that Donald was a sailor. Even he had no idea where they were when dawn broke. They landed on what they found was the Island of Benbecula, between North and South Uist, thankful to be still alive.

On this island the Prince was to spend some weeks, during which he made an adventurous passage to Stornoway and back, partly by sea, narrowly avoiding capture by an English ship, and partly on foot over the mountainous Isle of Lewis. Often in danger, he was never afraid of betrayal, although many hundreds of the islanders knew of his presence. Back in South Uist he lived dangerously in a hut invisible from the sea. Ten English ships were sailing up and down off the coast looking for him, and no doubt the Prince lay in the heather watching them. During all this time he moved from one miserable hiding place to another, but occasionally food and even a change of clothes were found for him.

One evening, possibly by chance, he came to a hut where a lady had gone to tend her brother's cattle. Flora MacDonald's name will never be forgotten so long as men are inspired by a story of gallant heroism and devotion.

After some natural hesitation, Flora MacDonald agreed to assist the Prince to cross to Skye, where her mother, also a loyal Jacobite, had a house close to the shore. There the fugitive could be safely hidden. South Uist having now become too dangerous for him, the need for a change was urgent.

Because it might be necessary to deceive English soldiers patrolling the coast of Skye, it was thought better to disguise the Prince as a woman servant of Flora MacDonald. The handsome features and long fair hair of the Prince lent themselves to the part very well. Unfortunately he was a poor actor. When wading through the shallow water of a stream, he lifted his skirts above his knees and was told that no Scottish maid would be so immodest; fording the next stream he let them trail in the water. It was then pointed out to him that no Scottish girl would be so daft. It was very difficult.

It was a stormy night as they crossed the Minch to Skye. As they drew near to the shore they were challenged by an English patrol and fired upon when they turned and rowed away. The English muskets of the period were not precision weapons and there were no casualties.

The Prince soon decided that as a girl he was not convincing. He changed back to male attire, and after another period of hiding in mountain huts, he crossed back to the mainland. There was no doubt that the risk would here be greater, but there would be more room to evade the enemy searching parties.

During the next eleven weeks the adventurous wanderings of the Prince, often through country devastated by Butcher Cumberland, sleeping in mountain huts or under the stars, were full of narrow escapes. Patrols passed within a few yards of where he was hiding, or he would lie on a hillside and watch the busy soldiers making camp in the valley below.

An English patrol fires upon them

On September the 19th, 1746, the Prince sailed in the French ship *L'Heureux*, from within a few yards of where he had landed so hopefully on July the 25th of the year before. One of the most romantic and reckless adventures in history had ended in desolation and ruin.

Prince Charles Edward reached the little French port of Roscoff, in Brittany, ten days later. He had hoped to obtain the help of France in another attempt at the invasion of England, but the French King had lost whatever faith he ever had in the chances of Prince Charles. Nor was there any possibility of raising another army in Scotland. Butcher Cumberland had done his evil work too well.

For two years the Prince remained in France, no doubt finding life in Paris more comfortable than in a deserted cow-shed in a Scottish glen. It was not to last. The French had had enough of war, and the English insisted, in the Treaty of Aix-la-Chapelle, that Prince Charles should no longer remain on French soil. Refusing to leave, he was for a short time imprisoned and finally, in December, taken to the French frontier and expelled.

For a few years he continued to appeal for help in France and England. Wandering about Europe, often in disguise and welcome nowhere, he never perhaps entirely lost hope. But 'Bonnie Prince Charlie' had gone for ever, except as the romantic hero of a legend of gay adventure. Sir Winston Churchill has supplied the epitaph. 'Jacobitism vanished from the political life of Great Britain, but Highland Regiments have brought glory to Scotland, and ever since have stood in the forefront of the British Army.'

Scottish soldiers are famous for their courage

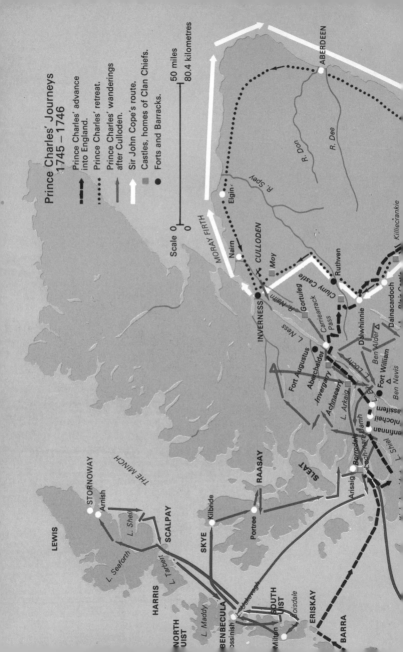

Prince Charles' Journeys
1745 – 1746

Prince Charles' advance into England.

Prince Charles' retreat.

Prince Charles' wanderings after Culloden.

Sir John Cope's route.

■ Castles, homes of Clan Chiefs.

● Forts and Barracks.

Scale 0   50 miles

0   80.4 kilometres

ABERDEEN

R. Don

R. Dee

R. Spey

Elgin

MORAY FIRTH

Nairn

CULLODEN

Moy

INVERNESS

Gortuleg

Carriearrack Pass

Cluny Castle

Ruthven

Dalwhinnie

Killiecrankie

L. Ness

Fort Augustus

Aberchalder

Ben Alder △

Dalnacardoch

Invergarry

L. Oich

L. Lochy

Fort William

Ben Nevis △

L. Arkaig

Achnacarry

Gortleck

R. Nairn

Glenfinnan

nlochmoidart

L. Shiel

Arisaig

Loch-nan-Uamh

Borrodale

STORNOWAY

Arnish

THE MINCH

LEWIS

L. Shell

L. Seaforth

HARRIS

L. Tarbert

SCALPAY

RAASAY

Kilbride

SKYE

Portree

SLEAT

NORTH UIST

L. Maddy

ssinish

BENBECULA

ttlehough

Ossinish

Milton

Oisdale

SOUTH UIST

ERISKAY

BARRA